I Am Bursting My Joy Over You

This book is a gift to:

_____

From:

_____

I know Jeanine's heart for God and her passion to see people come to know Him more deeply and intimately like she has.

Jeanine says it best in her own words when she writes: "I am calling you closer to Me. Do you hear my heartbeat?"

I can't think of a better way to spend a month of my time, then to leisurely mull over the meditations that Jeanine has downloaded from on high."

~ Rev. Karen L. Workentin ~
Dean Rhema Bible Training College Australia
Director Harvestime Ministries Inc.

Joy bursts through the words and the pictures of this delightful devotional book.

Over 28 days, Jeanine shares with us the joy she has discovered in God in times of difficulty, grief and loss.

I highly recommend you take this adoration journey and rediscover God's delight over you.

~ Andrew Chisholm ~
Senior Minister
CityLife Church

I am bursting my Joy over you

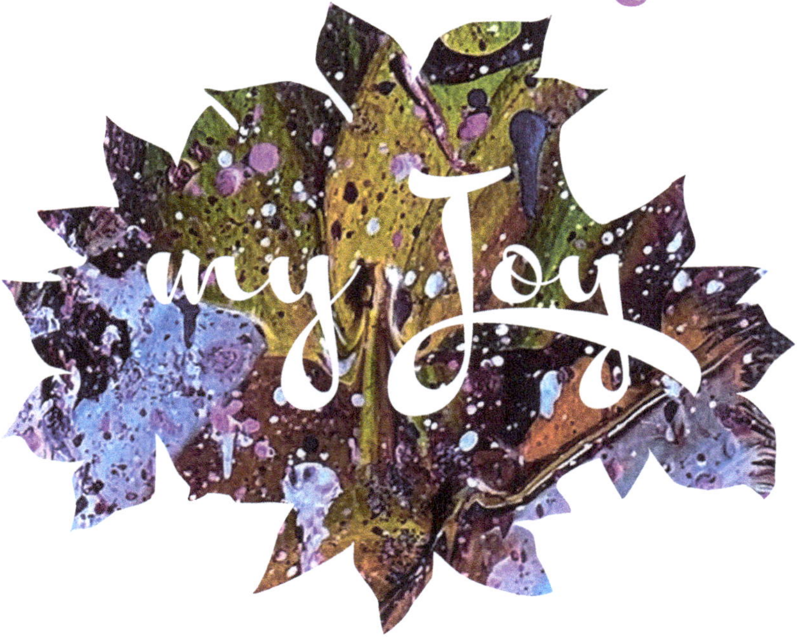

Jeanine Sharp

CARDINIA RANGES PUBLISHING HOUSE
Beaconsfield, Victoria 3807, Australia
cardiniaranges.com
info@cardiniaranges.com

I AM BURSTING MY JOY OVER YOU: Prophetic Adoration, Journal & Reflections
Copyright ©2022 by Jeanine Sharp
First published 2022

ALL RIGHTS RESERVED. Apart from any fair dealing for the purpose of private study, research, criticism or review, as permitted under the Copyright Act, no part may be reproduced by any process without written permission. Inquiries should be addressed to the publisher.

Cardinia Ranges Publishing House exists with the mission of inspiring people to fulfill their God-given potential.

SCRIPTURE QUOTATIONS are taken from the HOLY BIBLE, NEW LIVING TRANSLATION, copyright ©1996, 2004, 2015 by Tyndale House Foundation. Used by permission of Tyndale House Publishers, Carol Stream, Illinois 60188. All rights reserved.

A catalogue record for this book is available from the National Library of Australia

ISBN: 987-1-922537-05-8 (print edition)
ISBN: 987-1-922537-06-5 (Mobi & Kindle edition)

To my Dad

Although he would never agree, I received some of my creativity from him. He suddenly passed away two weeks after I wrote this Prophetic Adoration. I miss him a lot and catch my breath every time I create something and want to share it with him.

To Jim, my husband

Jim's parting words to me were: "Go live your best life!"

Writing this book is one of the many steps towards me honouring him and taking steps to living my best life.

Kangaroo Grass

Introduction

During one of my treasured moments of worship in May 2020, with Father God, I experienced like I was with Him in his throne room, being completely consumed by his love. I asked Father God: "I want to hear what you have on your heart?" Out of that most precious time came this work of worship, this Prophetic Adoration.

I wanted to encourage people from God's heart (it was during one of Melbourne's many and grim lockdowns related to the pandemic), so I created a manuscript from engaging with Scripture, but then from God's perspective.

Each of the reflections in this journal is based on this Prophetic Adoration and the accompanying Scripture verses. In line with the Prophetic Adoration itself, with each reflection I felt inspired to write them in such a way that Father God himself is speaking to you. Let Him speak to you and encourage you when you spend time with Him and engage with Him.

My heart's desire is for you to experience treasured moments with Father God's love. Let Him speak to you through this adoration and these reflections.

The best way to do this, is to find a place where you can sit somewhere comfortable and quiet. Here, you can read the encouraging word from Father God's heart to you. Then, reflect on what Father God is saying to you and what He is inviting you to. Lastly, take the time to write your experiences and thoughts in this journal. Allow these experiences to not be limited by a set time frame, so you can fully engage with Father God's love for you.

Throughout this book, you may also notice the simple splendour of Australian native flowers. I drew these for your enjoyment as you spend time with Father God.

~ Introduction ~

However, they are also dear to me personally as they reflect and honour the life of my husband Jim, who passed away in August 2021. Jim loved talking with Father God and spending time with him through nature and looking at the splendour of his creation. Now I want to bless you the same way with these expressions of God's creation.

Maybe you have experienced loss yourself? I want to encourage you then through these flowers and this Prophetic Adoration. The same way, Father God has always filled me and equipped me with His Joy and Love, while I received Peace from Jesus and comfort from the Holy Spirit.

I have freedom knowing my future is full of opportunities as I continue to take steps of faith in the journey Father God has prepared for me. And He has prepared a special journey for you, too.

I pray that, as you spend precious time with Father God and journey with Him, you enjoy these treasured moments and all that He has for you. May you be richly blessed through the experience of knowing his love for you.

Audiovisual Experience

This journal is complemented by the Prophetic Adoration of "I am bursting My Joy over you" audiovisual compilation. This compilation is accessible via this weblink:

https://cardiniaranges.com/books/I-am-bursting-my-joy-over-you/

Prophetic Adoration
I am bursting my Joy over you

> "I am bursting my Joy over you
>
> I will put praise on your lips
>
> I have freed you from your fears
>
> Drink deeply of my Goodness
>
> I am calling out to you
>
> Every morning, I fill you with my Joy
>
> I am your sanctuary, your hiding place
>
> My promises are for your pleasure
>
> My Favour is wrapped around you. You are covered under a canopy
>
> I look at you with passionate longing
>
> My heart is on fire and passion for you
>
> I am overflowing with words of a sacred story
>
> My elegant Grace pours over you when I speak
>
> You are clothed in my Glory and grandeur to go forth in victory
>
> My Faithfulness and Truth will cause you to stand

~ Introduction ~

I am a constant river flowing, whose sparkling streams bring you joy and delight

I want to illuminate your heart with light

I want you to experience the full revelation of the hope of my calling

I want you to know through experience the immeasurable greatness of my power made available to you

Let my fullness fill you

I want to unveil within you the unlimited riches of my Glory and Favour, to flood your innermost being with explosive power

Let my Love be the resting place and source in your life as you discover everything that I am for you

You are never alone; I am always with you. You are part of my sacred story

You are my child!"

~ Introduction ~

Day 1

I am bursting my Joy over you

Day 1

{ **THE FATHER SAYS TO YOU**

"I am bursting my Joy over you" }

HIS ENCOURAGEMENT

Everything I am, all of Me, has been given to you as an expression of my Joy.

My Joy breaks through barriers and fills you with strength to overcome.

HIS INVITATION

Quiet yourself in my presence and focus only on Me. Come and be with Me and find Me in the stillness.

Ask Me to fill you with my Joy. See yourself overcoming with Joy as the expression and write out your prayers and thoughts to me.

~ I Am Bursting My Joy Over You ~

With every bone in my body I will praise him: "Lord, who can compare with you? Who else rescues the helpless from the strong? Who else protects the helpless and poor from those who rob them?"

Psalm 35:10

~ I Am Bursting My Joy Over You ~

~ 14 ~

Day 2

{ **THE FATHER SAYS TO YOU**
"I will put praise on your lips " }

HIS ENCOURAGEMENT

Praising Me, releases my Joy into your soul and refreshes you.

Praising Me helps you to be aware of Me in you – as you are in my Son Jesus through my Holy Spirit.

Praising Me is thanking Me for all I have done for you as you recount my wonderful works.

HIS INVITATION

Praise Me, open your heart and share with Me your experience of my Love, my Tenderness, my Goodness, my Protection, my Blessing and my Joy.

Express what this praise feels like. How does it make you feel? How do you feel about Me?

~ I Will Put Praise On Your Lips ~

But give great joy to those who came to my defence. Let them continually say, "Great is the Lord, who delights in blessing his servant with peace!"

Psalm 35:27

~ I Will Put Praise On Your Lips ~

Day 3

I have freed you from your fears

Day 3

{ **THE FATHER SAYS TO YOU**
"I have freed you from your fears" }

HIS ENCOURAGEMENT

My Joy in you always overcomes all fear. You have nothing to fear because I am with you.

My Peace is full of my perfect Love. When you experience my Peace, you will also experience my Joy.

HIS INVITATION

Take now some time to breathe slowly and allow my Peace to cascade over you. My Peace is saturated in my Love.

Listen for my voice as you ask Me anything you want to know about Me. I will share with you all the intimate expressions of Love I have for you.

~ I Have Freed You From Your Fears ~

Then I will rejoice in the Lord. I will be glad because he rescues me.
Psalm 35:9

~ I Have Freed You From Your Fears ~

Day 4

Drink deeply of my Goodness

Day 4

{ **THE FATHER SAYS TO YOU**

"Drink deeply of my Goodness" }

HIS ENCOURAGEMENT

When you enter into my Presence, you drink deeply of my Goodness. My Goodness overflows from my Joy fountain. Everything you need comes from my Goodness.

My Joy breaks through barriers and fills you with strength to overcome.

HIS INVITATION

Believe Me that you are full of my Goodness. In every part of your being. In every breath you take. Meditate on this for a moment...

What does it look like to be full of my Goodness? What does it feel like?

~ Drink Deeply Of My Goodness ~

O Lord, you know all about this. Do not stay silent. Do not abandon me now, O Lord.

Psalm 35:22

~ Drink Deeply Of My Goodness ~

Day 5

{ **THE FATHER SAYS TO YOU**

"I am calling out to you" }

HIS ENCOURAGEMENT

I am calling out to you in every sunrise. I am waking up a new day for you, which is filled with my Joy and splendour.

My voice is gentle and knowing; it speaks of truth. I speak into your mind, and in many ways my voice sounds just like yours. I am calling you closer to Me. Do you hear my heartbeat?

HIS INVITATION

Beloved, steady yourself and find rest. Hold captive every thought to the obedience of Christ. Think of all things lovely and pure, and of my grandeur. Ask Me about how I see you.

~ I Am Calling Out To You ~

Listen to my cry for help, my King and my God, for I pray to no one but you. Listen to my voice in the morning, Lord. Each morning I bring my requests to you and wait expectantly.

Psalm 5:2–3

~ I Am Calling Out To You ~

Day 6

Every morning, I fill you with my Joy

Day 6

{ **THE FATHER SAYS TO YOU** }
{ "Every morning, I fill you with my Joy" }

HIS ENCOURAGEMENT

Every day is a new day where I can gaze upon you with Joy. Every day, my delight is to fill you with my Joy and to watch you share it with others.

I am delighted with Joy, when you show others my Grace and blessings through your words and actions.

HIS INVITATION

Sweet child of mine, you are a Joy to behold like a rising sunrise. Just as the day awakens and light explodes... It was like this the very moment you entered into my Glory and you were awakened with light, through my Son Jesus!

Share with Me, how did it feel for you to be filled with Light?

~ Every Morning, I Fill You With My Joy ~

Listen to my voice in the morning, Lord. Each morning I bring my requests to you and wait expectantly.

Psalm 5:3

~ Every Morning, I Fill You With My Joy ~

Day 7

Reflection from Days 1-6

Day 7

{ **THE FATHER HAS BEEN SAYING TO YOU** }

"I am bursting my Joy over you
I will put praise on your lips
I have freed you from your fears
Drink deeply of my Goodness
I am calling out to you
Every morning, I fill you with my Joy"

REFLECTION

Write a letter to Father God about how the journey of discovering his Joy for you has burst forth. How He showed it to you more exceedingly and abundantly than what you could have imagined or hoped!

~ REFLECTION FROM DAYS 1–6 ~

Now all glory to God, who is able, through his mighty power at work within us, to accomplish infinitely more than we might ask or think.

EPHESIANS 3:20

~ Reflection From Days 1–6 ~

Day 8

> **THE FATHER SAYS TO YOU**
>
> "I am your sanctuary, your hiding place"

HIS ENCOURAGEMENT

Be still and know that I am God. Hide away in Me, in my amazing Love, my exuberant Grace and richest Mercy. Come and hide in Me above all your cares and troubles, and I will fill you with my Joy to strengthen you to overcome.

HIS INVITATION

Beloved, develop the practice of rest. Think about Me with every breath you take. I am with you always. Together we walk through the valley hand in hand.

You are hidden in Me; I am a shield wrapped around you. What does your shield look like? What does it feel like?

~ I Am Your Sanctuary, Your Hiding Place ~

Because of your unfailing love, I can enter your house; I will worship at your Temple with deepest awe.

Psalm 5:7

~ I Am Your Sanctuary, Your Hiding Place ~

Day 9

My promises are for your pleasure

Day 9

{ **THE FATHER SAYS TO YOU**

"My promises are for your pleasure" }

HIS ENCOURAGEMENT

Everything I am and everything I created is for your delight. I am everything you need.

My Son is my greatest pleasure and it pleased Me to offer Him as a living sacrifice for you, so you could experience my Joy and my promises.

HIS INVITATION

Consider *my* Son Jesus, and the Joy it was for Me to send Him to be your living sacrifice, so you could be with Me.

Commune with Me for a while, become aware of how you are in my Son Jesus and how Jesus remains in you.

Express to Me what you are experiencing in this moment.

The law of Moses was unable to save us because of the weakness of our sinful nature. So God did what the law could not do. He sent his own Son in a body like the bodies we sinners have. And in that body God declared an end to sin's control over us by giving his Son as a sacrifice for our sins.

Romans 8:3

~ My Promises Are For Your Pleasure ~

Day 10

My Favour is wrapped around you. You are covered under a canopy

Day 10

THE FATHER SAYS TO YOU

"My Favour is wrapped around you.
You are covered under a canopy"

HIS ENCOURAGEMENT

My delight is for you to know how much I adore you and Favour you. My Favour offers you a confident rest in my Goodness. My Favour is like a shield that covers you from every weapon formed against you. It brings Me great Joy to pour out my Favour upon you as you walk with Me and know Me.

HIS INVITATION

Humble yourself before Me and seek Me with all of your heart. Seek Me for Wisdom in every situation you face. In what area in your life, do you need my Favour? Do you need my Protection, my Rest, my Goodness or my Joy?

~ My Favour Is Wrapped Around You. You Are Covered Under A Canopy ~

For you bless the godly, O Lord; you surround them with your shield of love.
Psalm 5:12

~ My Favour Is Wrapped Around You. You Are Covered Under A Canopy ~

Day 11

I look at you with passionate longing

Day 11

{ ### THE FATHER SAYS TO YOU
"I look at you with passionate longing" }

HIS ENCOURAGEMENT

I am the beholder of your beauty. I look at you with passionate longing pouring out into you, my Grace and Mercy. When I look at everything I have created, it is good. However, when I gaze upon you, it is very good and brings Me so much Joy!

HIS INVITATION

Look around you at all the things that I have created for you to enjoy. Look at the detail of it all: the intricate details of colour, size, shape, and use.

Pick a flower and write about what you see. Reflect upon this truth: when I look upon you, I see you are very good.

~ I Look At You With Passionate Longing ~

We keep looking to the Lord our God for his mercy, just as servants keep their eyes on their master, as a slave girl watches her mistress for the slightest signal.

Psalm 123:2

~ I Look At You With Passionate Longing ~

Day 12

My heart is on fire and passion for you

Day 12

{ THE FATHER SAYS TO YOU
"My heart is on fire and passion for you" }

HIS ENCOURAGEMENT

Every day my passion of Joy and Wonder is displayed through my Love for you. My heart is an all-consuming fire, that ignites hope and desire within you through Jesus.

HIS INVITATION

If you have lost hope about something, come before Me. Allow Me to ignite you again with my passion of Joy and Wonder. I will give you new hope and desire to accomplish the plans, purposes and promises I have for you.

~ My Heart Is On Fire And Passion For You ~

Beautiful words stir my heart. I will recite a lovely poem about the king, for my tongue is like the pen of a skilful poet.

Psalm 45:1

~ My Heart Is On Fire And Passion For You ~

Day 13

I am overflowing with words of a sacred story

Kangaroo Grass

Day 13

THE FATHER SAYS TO YOU

"I am overflowing with words of a sacred story"

HIS ENCOURAGEMENT

I love you so much. My Son Jesus is a living sacrifice for you. Jesus' sacred story flows towards you and overflows you through my words expressed with Love and Joy. My words continually flow from my heart to yours, always full of encouragement, strength, and comfort.

HIS INVITATION

Place your hand on your heart and receive the words with which I want to overflow you.

Welcome Jesus' sacred story for you. How does this feel? Write this down.

~ I Am Overflowing With Words Of A Sacred Story ~

You are the most handsome of all. Gracious words stream from your lips.
God himself has blessed you forever.

Psalm 45:2

~ I Am Overflowing With Words Of A Sacred Story ~

Day 14

Reflection from Days 8-13

Day 14

{ THE FATHER HAS BEEN SAYING TO YOU }

"I am your sanctuary, your hiding place

My promises are for your pleasure

My Favour is wrapped around you. You are covered under a canopy

I look at you with passionate longing

My heart is on fire and passion for you

I am overflowing with words of a sacred story"

REFLECTION

Write a letter to Father God about how the journey of discovering His Joy for you has burst forth. How He showed it to you more exceedingly and abundantly than what you could have imagined or hoped!

~ REFLECTION FROM DAYS 8–13 ~

For who can know the Lord's thoughts? Who knows enough to give him advice?

ROMANS 11:34

~ Reflection from Days 8–13 ~

Day 15

My elegant Grace pours over you when I speak

Day 15

{ **THE FATHER SAYS TO YOU**

"My elegant Grace pours over you when I speak" }

HIS ENCOURAGEMENT

I long to whisper words filled with elegance of refined beauty and my Grace. You are anointed with my splendour and Joy. You are highly favoured and graceful!

HIS INVITATION

Listen quietly for my whispers. Allow my words to wash over you and minister to you.

Gaze upon my Goodness of splendour in your life. Where has my splendour helped you to have Favour or Grace?

~ My Elegant Grace Pours Over You When I Speak ~

You are the most handsome of all. Gracious words stream from your lips.
God himself has blessed you forever.

Psalm 45:2

~ My Elegant Grace Pours Over You When I Speak ~

Day 16

You are clothed in my Glory and grandeur to go forth in victory

Day 16

{ **THE FATHER SAYS TO YOU**

"You are clothed in my Glory
and grandeur to go forth in victory" }

HIS ENCOURAGEMENT

I want to clothe you with my full expression of splendour towards you that you may experience the height, depth, length, and breadth of my Love for you. When you are clothed in Me, you have victory over every situation. When my Glory is wrapped around you, you shine with my Joy!

HIS INVITATION

From the top of your head to the bottom of your feet, allow Me to clothe you with my Glory.

Can you see my splendour? Can you experience my grandeur? Can you feel my Love?

Can you describe what these clothes look or feel like?

~ You Are Clothed In My Glory And Grandeur To Go Forth In Victory ~

In your majesty, ride out to victory, defending truth, humility, and justice.
Go forth to perform awe-inspiring deeds!

Psalm 45:4

~ You Are Clothed In My Glory And Grandeur To Go Forth In Victory ~

Day 17

My Faithfulness and Truth will cause you to stand

Day 17

{ **THE FATHER SAYS TO YOU**

"My Faithfulness and Truth
will cause you to stand" }

HIS ENCOURAGEMENT

You are my Child in whom I am well pleased! You excite Me when you believe my Truth and grow your Faith in Me. I become so excited when I strengthen you to stand strong in Me and allow me to fight for you.

HIS INVITATION

Is there something for which you need strength? Is there something for which you need to believe Me? Maybe there is something you can't do for yourself?

I would love to help you. Call out to Me and let Me do what I love to do for you.

~ My Faithfulness And Truth Will Cause You To Stand ~

In your majesty, ride out to victory, defending truth, humility, and justice.
Go forth to perform awe-inspiring deeds!

Psalm 45:4

~ My Faithfulness And Truth Will Cause You To Stand ~

Day 18

I am a constant river flowing, whose sparkling streams bring you joy and delight

Day 18

THE FATHER SAYS TO YOU

"I am a constant river flowing, whose sparkling streams bring you joy and delight"

HIS ENCOURAGEMENT

My streams are full of everything that is good! They flow straight from Me to you! My rivers will fill you up with the waters of my Kingdom.

My desire is for my rivers to overflow you in an expression of my kingdom language. Let them continually nourish you and bring you joy and delight.

HIS INVITATION

Allow Me to fill you up right now with my kingdom water flowing from my stream. When you feel full, allow this river to bubble up and overflow, by speaking out what comes upon your tongue.

My Peace is all you need right now. Don't strive, just relax and allow my Holy Spirit to do what He does well. My Joy will be experienced in new ways and expressed through tears and laughter. Keep going you are doing great!

What are you feeling? What are you sensing? Share this experience on these pages, so you can remember this day with Me.

~ I Am A Constant River Flowing, Whose Sparkling Streams Bring You Joy And Delight ~

A river brings joy to the city of our God, the sacred home of the Most High.
Psalm 46:4

~ I Am A Constant River Flowing, Whose Sparkling Streams Bring You Joy And Delight ~

Day 19

I want to illuminate your heart with light

Day 19

THE FATHER SAYS TO YOU

"I want to illuminate your heart with light"

HIS ENCOURAGEMENT

I created special lights for the day and the night... but I also created a unique light for you to carry. This light comes from my Son Jesus. He is the Light of the World, and his light is in you when you accept Him. When you live your life in obedience to Jesus and his promises, your light begins to shine brightly.

HIS INVITATION

Take a moment right now to reflect and think about how Jesus' light could shine brightly in you?

~ I Want To Illuminate Your Heart With Light ~

I pray that your hearts will be flooded with light so that you can understand the confident hope he has given to those he called – his holy people who are his rich and glorious inheritance.

Ephesians 1:18

~ I Want To Illuminate Your Heart With Light ~

Day 20

I want you to experience the full revelation of the hope of my calling

Native Oregano

Day 20

THE FATHER SAYS TO YOU

"I want you to experience the full revelation of the hope of my calling"

HIS ENCOURAGEMENT

When I created you, I created you in my own image. I knew who you were going to be and who you would become. I already know what you will achieve in your life. Therefore, my hope is for you to receive our plans for you as they are revealed.

HIS INVITATION

Rest in my Peace and Love for you. Ask Me about my plans for your life. Ask Me about whether there is anything you need to stop or start doing.

~ I Want You To Experience The Full Revelation Of The Hope Of My Calling ~

I pray that your hearts will be flooded with light so that you can understand the confident hope he has given to those he called – his holy people who are his rich and glorious inheritance.

Ephesians 1:18

~ I Want You To Experience The Full Revelation Of The Hope Of My Calling ~

Native Oregano

Day 21

Reflection from Days 15-20

Native Pigface

Day 21

THE FATHER HAS BEEN SAYING TO YOU

"My elegant Grace pours over you when I speak

You are clothed in my Glory and grandeur to go forth in victory

My Faithfulness and Truth will cause you to stand

I am a constant river flowing, whose sparkling streams bring you joy and delight

I want to illuminate your heart with light

I want you to experience

the full revelation of the hope of my calling"

REFLECTION

Write a letter to Father God about how the journey of discovering His Joy for you has burst forth. How He showed it to you more exceedingly and abundantly than what you could have imagined or hoped!

~ REFLECTION FROM DAYS 15–20 ~

Great is the LORD! He is most worthy of praise! No one can measure his greatness.

PSALM 145:3

~ Reflection From Days 15–20 ~

Day 22

I want you to know
through experience
the immeasurable
greatness of my power
made available to you

Day 22

THE FATHER SAYS TO YOU

{ "I want you to know through experience the immeasurable greatness of my power made available to you" }

HIS ENCOURAGEMENT

Every day I desire for you to ask Me, what the plan is for your day. I have treasures full of favour and grace for you to experience. I also have things for which you need to trust and fight with the Faith I have given you to succeed.

HIS INVITATION

Is there an area or situation in which you need my power to be made available to you?

What area in your life would you like my immeasurable Love to cascade into?

~ I Want You To Know Through Experience The Immeasurable Greatness Of My Power Made Available To You ~

I also pray that you will understand the incredible greatness of God's power for us who believe him. This is the same mighty power that raised Christ from the dead and seated him in the place of honor at God's right hand in the heavenly realms.

EPHESIANS 1:19–20

~ I Want You To Know Through Experience The Immeasurable Greatness Of My Power Made Available To You ~

Day 23

{ **THE FATHER SAYS TO YOU**

"Let my fullness fill you" }

HIS ENCOURAGEMENT

Everything I am and everything I have created is for you! I am always full of everything you need. I am never dry or empty. I am always full and ready to pour out into you anything that you need or desire.

HIS INVITATION

To know Me as Father, is to seek Me. What do you need from Me today? Allow Me to fill you up so much, that you experience the full measure of my Love for you.

~ Let My Fullness Fill You ~

God has put all things under the authority of Christ and has made him head over all things for the benefit of the church. And the church is his body; it is made full and complete by Christ, who fills all things everywhere with himself.

Ephesians 1:22–23

~ Let My Fullness Fill You ~

Day 24

I want to unveil within you the unlimited riches of my Glory and Favour, to flood your innermost being with explosive power

Day 24

THE FATHER SAYS TO YOU

{ "I want to unveil within you the unlimited riches of my Glory and Favour, to flood your innermost being with explosive power" }

HIS ENCOURAGEMENT

When you are full of my Love, you are full of my immeasurable riches. The more you seek Me, the more Favour I can show you.

HIS INVITATION

Quietly ponder on how full you are of my Glory in the innermost parts of your being.

Is there any area of your being in which you need my explosive power? Seek Me and ask Me.

~ I Want To Unveil Within You The Unlimited Riches Of My Glory And Favour ~

I pray that from his glorious, unlimited resources he will empower you with inner strength through his Spirit.

EPHESIANS 3:16

~ I Want To Unveil Within You The Unlimited Riches Of My Glory And Favour ~

Day 25

Let my Love be the resting place and source in your life as you discover everything that I am for you

Day 25

THE FATHER SAYS TO YOU

"Let my Love be the resting place and source in your life as you discover everything that I am for you"

HIS ENCOURAGEMENT

My Son Jesus now sits at my right hand with Me on my throne. He desires for you to rest in his finished work of the Cross, so you can enjoy being with Him right next to Me.

HIS INVITATION

Come and sit with Me in the throne room.

Take a moment to think about and experience being with my Son who sits right next to Me. What do you experience right now? What goes through your mind and your body?

~ Let My Love Be The Resting Place And Source In Your Life As You Discover Everything That I Am For You ~

Then Christ will make his home in your hearts as you trust in him. Your roots will grow down into God's love and keep you strong.

Ephesians 3:17

~ Let My Love Be The Resting Place And Source In Your Life As You Discover Everything That I Am For You ~

Day 26

You are never alone; I am always with you. You are part of my sacred story

Day 26

THE FATHER SAYS TO YOU

"You are never alone; I am always with you. You are part of my sacred story"

HIS ENCOURAGEMENT

Beloved Child, my Joy is to know that you are with Me in my secret place. Here, I can adore you and enjoy you, as you live your life with Me and my Son Jesus who lives through you. My delight is knowing that you trust Me and believe Me.

HIS INVITATION

Write Me a letter about how this Journey of discovering my Joy for you has burst forth exceedingly and far more abundantly than what you could have imagined or hoped!

~ You Are Never Alone; I Am Always With You. You Are Part Of My Sacred Story ~

And may you have the power to understand, as all God's people should, how wide, how long, how high, and how deep his love is. May you experience the love of Christ, though it is too great to understand fully. Then you will be made complete with all the fullness of life and power that comes from God.

EPHESIANS 3:18–19

~ You Are Never Alone; I Am Always With You. You Are Part Of My Sacred Story ~

Day 27

THE FATHER SAYS TO YOU

"You are my child!"

HIS ENCOURAGEMENT

My precious child, because of you putting your faith in the faithfulness of my Son Jesus, through Him you have now been accepted into my family. You are fully immersed into Love, and you are covered and clothed with Jesus' life and anointing.

HIS INVITATION

Take some time to awaken every part of you to become fully immersed in my Love right now. Express your love and appreciation of what this means for you?

Share with Me how you feel about being my child?

~ You Are My Child! ~

For you are all children of God through faith in Christ Jesus. And all who have been united with Christ in baptism have put on Christ, like putting on new clothes.

Galatians 3:26–27

~ You Are My Child! ~

Day 28

Reflection from Days 22-27

Day 28

THE FATHER HAS BEEN SAYING TO YOU

"I want you to know through experience the immeasurable greatness of my power made available to you

Let my fullness fill you

I want to unveil within you the unlimited riches of my Glory and Favour, to flood your innermost being with explosive power

Let my Love be the resting place and source in your life as you discover everything that I am for you

You are never alone; I am always with you.

You are part of my sacred story

You are my child!"

REFLECTION

Write a letter to Father God about how the journey of discovering His Joy for you has burst forth. How He showed it to you more exceedingly and abundantly than what you could have imagined or hoped!

~ Reflection From Days 22–27 ~

I am overwhelmed with joy in the Lord my God! For he has dressed me with the clothing of salvation and draped me in a robe of righteousness. I am like a bridegroom dressed for his wedding or a bride with her jewels.

Isaiah 61:10

~ Reflection From Days 22–27 ~

About the Author

Originally from the Australian state of Queensland, Jeanine now lives in Melbourne where she actively serves in her local church. Jeanine enjoys being creative in many ways, among these are prophetic art and creating colourful abstract designs using acrylic paints on canvas. She really is passionate about developing her unique voice to engage with Father God through prophetic adoration.

Jeanine pursues an intimate relationship with Father God and seeks to advance the Kingdom of God in a purposeful way through prayer. She has a passion to encourage people to hear the voice of God for themselves, and to inspire others to develop their own relationship with God, pursuing Father God's promises.

Jeanine is honoured to be a mother to three adult children and one daughter-in-law. Each of these have served as missionaries around the world, sharing their relationship with Father God and belief in Jesus as their Lord and Saviour, and now enjoy serving at their churches.

Acknowledgements

I would like to acknowledge my children and say "thank you". Madeleine, thank you for being compassionate, tolerant, patient, and genuine. Thank you for all the support you have given me and for helping me to believe, that anything is possible. You have Blessed me so much. Mathew and Kortney, thank you for listening to all of the ideas, plans, dreams, and each step of creating this book, I have appreciated your encouragement. Braydan, you have kept me grounded, to stay focused, and to stay true to what I believe. You have inspired me to make changes in my thinking to live a better life. To Dean and Adam, you will always be part of my family and I will always have time to be with you. You all have a special place in my heart, and I treasure you all so much! Love you heaps and Bless you more.

www.ingramcontent.com/pod-product-compliance
Lightning Source LLC
Chambersburg PA
CBHW040241130526
44590CB00049B/4134